Devoted to all Enlightened Masters

19 Big Secrets About Astro Gems

Heinz Krug
Robert Thurston

2nd Edition

Published by:

Heinz Krug, drheinz@birthtime.info

Robert Thurston, vediccrystal@gmx.co.uk

Distributed by Lightning Source, UK/USA

Copyright © 2011,2012,2013 Heinz Krug, Robert Thurston.
All rights reserved.

ISBN: 978-0-9854241-6-9

Disclaimer:

This book is not intended as a substitute for the medical advice of physicians. The reader should regularly consult a physician in matters relating to his/her health and particularly with respect to any symptoms that may require diagnosis or medical attention.

Although the authors and publisher have made every effort to ensure that the information in this book was correct at the time of going to press, the authors and publisher do not assume, and hereby disclaim any liability to any party for any loss, damage, or disruption caused by errors or omissions, whether such errors or omissions result from negligence, accident, or any other cause.

Table of Contents

19 BIG SECRETS ABOUT ASTRO GEMS..................................III
ACKNOWLEDGMENTS..VII

Secret 1
  THE LIFE CHANGING EFFECTS OF WEARING GEMS.....................1

Secret 2
  USE ORIGINAL JYOTISH RATHER THAN WESTERN ASTROLOGY.....5

Secret 3
  USE YOUR INDIVIDUAL BIRTH CHART..8

Secret 4
  CHOOSE YOUR DESTINY WITH RELOCATION...............................11

Secret 5
  EFFECTS OF GEMS ON THE AURA..14

Secret 6
  GEMS FOR THE NINE PLANETARY QUANTUM FIELDS..................17

Secret 7
  THE STORY OF THE CREATION OF NATURAL GEMS....................20

Secret 8
  OUT OF THE GROUND OR FROM THE LAB?.................................22

Secret 9
  AVOID TREATED NATURAL GEMS...29

Secret 10
  HOW TO FULFILL YOUR DESIRES...32

Secret 11
  SELECTION METHOD: STRENGTHEN POSITIVE, NOT NEGATIVE...35

Secret 12
    GEM COMBINATIONS..38
Secret 13
    THE SQUARE LAW: SIZE DOES MATTER.............................41
Secret 14
    INCREASE THE SIZE OVER TIME....................................43
Secret 15
    DO NOT HAVE IT TOO BIG..45
Secret 16
    HOW TO WEAR GEMS..47
Secret 17
    WHEN TO WEAR GEMS...50
Secret 18
    RELIEF OF NOT WEARING THE WRONG GEMS OR METALS........52
Secret 19
    INCREASE YOUR CONSCIOUSNESS..................................55
Contact
    AUTHORS..59
    WEBSITE..59
Appendix 1
    WEIGHT MEASURES..60
Appendix 2
    JEWELS..61
Appendix 3
    SANSKRIT NAMES OF VARIOUS GEMS...............................64

Acknowledgments

The authors would like to thank Peter Westbrook, Gina Westbrook and Simon Best (caduceus.info) for their truly amazing help and assistance, their proofreading and deep discussions.

Secret 1

The Life Changing Effects of Wearing Gems

As we enter the 21st century, we can reveal for the first time in this modern age a complete understanding of the secret effects of *Jyotish* and *Jyotish* gemstones.

We shall reveal to you the original descriptions, lost for thousands of years, of a highly advanced Vedic civilization that could change its destiny. Vedic peoples believed that at the core of their physical being was the light of life itself, an ever-resounding vibration of light and sound that creates our universe and each one of us.

Using the highly systematic Sanskrit language, and combining astronomy, astrology and astro-relocation, this ancient Vedic culture preserved the exact formulas used to calculate planetary quantum fields. The resulting science, known as *Jyotish* – which is Sanskrit for light – included descriptions of the abilities of gemstones to change a person's destiny based on the cosmic laws governing our universe.

The basic formulas of *Jyotish* describe nine planetary quantum fields representing sound and light, in a spectrum similar to the seven frequency colors of the rainbow (red, orange, yellow, green, blue, indigo and violet) plus one for infra-red (IR) and one for ultraviolet (UV) light. These nine quantum fields are the source of our environment and influence all life on the planet and our solar system. They govern our lives much more than scientists have previously believed. But now, several researchers, such as Prof. Fritz

Popp in Germany, have confirmed that photons of light are emitted by every living cell.

Prof. Popp observed that particles of light, known as biophotons, are emitted by all living cells. It is a vital discovery as it appears that this light is essential in the functioning of the nervous system and other communications systems in all living organisms. The light, originally absorbed from the sun, is emitted coherently, as in a laser. With many sources of such light existing within the very large DNA molecules, it suggests the creation of a hologram as these streams of coherent light interact. Such a hologram, emanating from the DNA, would supply the structural information and act as a catalyst for the chemical reactions taking place within the cells. The gross body, arising from chemical interactions, forms around the subtle body, consisting of three-dimensional laser holograms, a process modern genetic science does not come close to comprehending.

These projections of coherent light are also essential to cell repair, and thus to health and longevity. Further, in repair mode, the frequency of the light is critical: cells absorb very specific frequencies from the total frequency spectrum of sunlight. If these frequencies are blocked, cell repair is prevented. This points the way to the medicine of the future, while reviving ancient knowledge from Vedic times. More to the point here, *correctly chosen gems influence the wavelengths of sun light that enter and influence our physiology, and thus our destiny.* The source of the information required to select the gems? A correctly calculated Vedic birth chart.

Real Life Testimonial

Lab-created ruby 112 carat set in gold

A scientist received a large, 112-carat, lab-created ruby, and from the first day of wearing it experienced clear changes in his life. The gem was meant to create more fame for this scientist, a 50-year-old man who had never been in the lime light. Within hours of wearing the gem for the first time, he and his sister – with her 24-carat ruby – were strolling around a little town and passed an ice cream parlor. It was a sunny spring day and a local TV station was shooting some footage, looking for nice people buying ice cream. That evening local TV viewers saw brother and sister enjoying their ice cream. Instant fame with a sweet taste!

This was only the beginning, however. In the following months, with the ruby enlivening his mind, he carried out many new, deep discoveries through which he secured even more lasting fame.

Quote

"Astrology is the study of man's response to planetary stimuli. The stars have no conscious benevolence or animosity; they merely send forth positive and negative radiations. Of themselves, these do not help or harm humanity, but offer a lawful channel for the outward operation of cause-effect equilibriums which each man has set into motion in the past."

Paramahansa Yogananda

Secret 1 Summary

Jyotish, or Vedic Astrology, is an ancient science very compatible with modern science. It is based on how the dynamics of the solar system influence quantum fields.

Solar System Quantum Fields – an artist's impression

Secret 2

Use Original Jyotish Rather than Western Astrology

Astronomy, which stands at the origin of modern science, owes an enormous debt to astrology. Some of the earliest western scientists, such as Galileo Galilei and Johannes Kepler, were actually astrologers. Indeed, at times, Kepler made his living casting horoscopes. It was their struggle, in the early 17th century, to make science independent of religious authorities, that laid the foundation for modern astronomy.

Unfortunately, even today, astronomy rejects astrology. Astronomy appears like an adult and, seemingly, self-sufficient son still struggling for his freedom against his father.

In reality, the father has a wealth of experience that is more than 5,000 years old. Therefore we recommend using this original astrology known as *Jyotish*, or Vedic astrology. Vedic comes from *Veda*, the Sanskrit word for knowledge. Jyotish is Sanskrit for light.

What are the advantages of this original system of astrology?

Jyotish is far more accurate than any western system of astrology. When an individual horoscope is calculated from correct data – such as birth date, birth time and birth place – future predictions can be accurate to within a day. While western astrology tends to focus on descriptions of character of a person, accurate predictions are not its strength. *Jyotish* characterizes life events; it explains the fundamental causal factors leading to events that occur at specific times in the life of the individual. It also provides the degree of accuracy essential for the correct selection and recommendation of gems.

The greater accuracy of *Jyotish* arises from its use of the sidereal zodiac, as opposed to the tropical zodiac used by most western astrological systems. The sidereal zodiac comprises the real star constellations that can be see in the night sky. Apart from some tiny fluctuations, these constellations are immovable over thousands of years. The tropical zodiac, by contrast, moves across the heavens, following the precession of the equinoxes.

The sidereal and tropical zodiacs coincided about 1,700 years ago – exactly on 5th November, 285 – but since that time the tropical zodiac has slowly drifted away. As a result, today they are more than 24° apart – exactly 24°00'00" on 4th December, 2009. This is a very large discrepancy; it is responsible for many inaccuracies in non-Vedic astrological systems. Slowly, over the centuries, western astrology has developed more into a belief system than the accurate science which *Jyotish* has been and still is today.

In fact, western astrology developed from Vedic astrology. Probably the knowledge traveled along ancient trading routes, initially from India to Mesopotamia/Babylonia. It contributed to the foundations of Byzantine and medieval Islamic astrology, before arriving in Greece from where it spread throughout Europe, and later to America. It is very possible, however, that a great deal of the knowledge – perhaps 80% to 90% – was lost en route. If one compares Vedic to western astrology, clearly there are some similarities, but the differences are considerable.

There have been several scientific evaluations of the validity of astrology. Unfortunately these have been done on western astrology. These researches have always demonstrated that the claims of western astrology are untrue and, even in the best cases, statistically insignificant.

It may astonish you, but we completely agree. Now we ask those scientists to redo their researches and examine what we call a science, namely Vedic astrology.

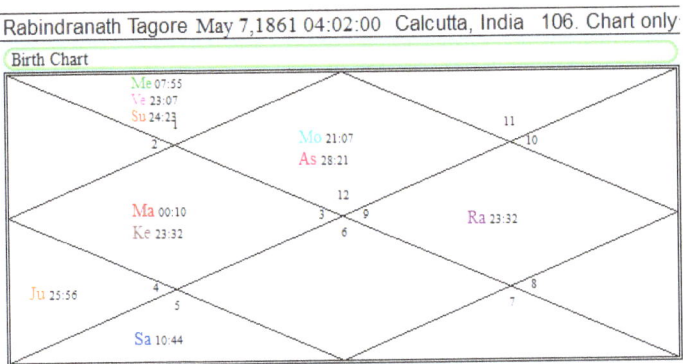

Example of a Vedic Astrology Chart, Janma Kundali

Real Life Testimonial

The editor of a UK alternative magazine dealing with western astrology obtained an 18-carat blue sapphire that was selected for him by a Vedic astrologer. Within a year he had taken over the magazine as the new owner, and is now distributing his magazine world-wide.

Quote

"Everything in life is predictable. Everything can be predicted from one point through Vedic Mathematics, or Jyotish."

Maharishi Mahesh Yogi, press conference, 9th August 2006

Secret 2 Summary

The original Vedic astrology is far more precise than later systems, both for predicting life events and for recommending appropriate gems.

Secret 3

Use Your Individual Birth Chart

No two people are the same. Even twins born only a few seconds or minutes apart will have somewhat different destinies. Their lives, passions, careers and attitudes will differ. You can locate those differences in their individual horoscopes as long as you enter their proper birth time – the exact second of their first breath – accurately to the second. With this first breath, an individual starts to interact with the Earth's environment, and will continue to do so until the last breath.

From this exact time of birth, a Vedic astrologer can calculate the timing of good opportunities for love, success, happiness, money, and career. Once you know the calendar of all those good opportunities ahead of time, you will be able to plan for the changes you wish. With such a unique knowledge, you can become the master of your own destiny. Properly chosen gems can help you achieve this goal. However, a birth stone chosen purely according to your birth month does not have any useful effect. There are only 12 months in a year and 12 zodiac constellations, but there are billions of types of people on the planet, so an accurate horoscope has to be more specific. It has to be done individually based on four factors:

1) Birth date

2) Birth time

3) Birth place

4) Current place of residence *

* The influence of your place of residence on your gem selection will be dealt with in more detail in the next chapter

Real Life Testimonial

19 carat lab-ruby

A beautiful and intelligent 49-year-old German lady was always interested in astrology and gems. She started to collect gems in wonderful jewelry boxes at home. When she first showed her collection to her Vedic astrologer, he admired her treasures, but also recommended that she start wearing the gems immediately. Only from this, would the effects start to manifest.

He recommended that she start with a 24-carat lab-created ruby. She followed his advice, and exceptional changes began to happen in her life. Her health improved and she was given more interesting tasks at work which she found very fulfilling.

Quote

"Anyone can be a millionaire, but to become a billionaire, you need an astrologer."

J. P. Morgan, famous banker and industrialist

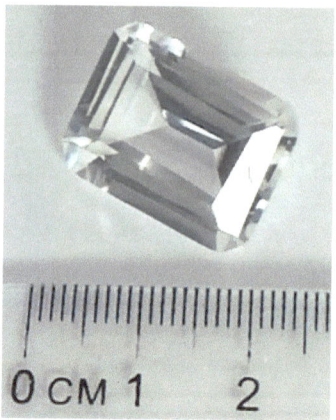
Lab-created, 29 carat white sapphire

Secret 3 Summary

Every individual is unique. This uniqueness can only be found in an individual horoscope calculated on accurate birth data, including place of residence.

48 carat, blue lab sapphire

Secret 4

Choose Your Destiny with Relocation

When you were born, certain star and planet constellations were visible in the sky. You may have been born at sunrise, for example. The sunrise in the east occurs only at certain places at a given time. All other places had another angle to the Sun. Some had the Sun in the West, some in the zenith straight above, some had the Sun invisible at night.

Depending on the angle of the Sun, Moon and planets during your birth time, you will experience different destinies in different locations on Planet Earth. This actually means moving around on the globe can change your destiny.

We have observed this phenomenon thousands of times: people who have traveled to another place on the globe experience events that could not be read from their original horoscopes based on their place of birth. These new events have occurred simply as a result of the relocation, which becomes very clear once one applies the horoscope based on the new location.

For example, some couples have found it difficult having children in their birthplace, but once they relocated they had several children. The same applies to career changes, income, wealth, health, happiness – basically all factors of destiny.

Gems allow you to improve your destiny in different places on Earth. They are selected to strengthen positive planetary influences. The angles of Sun, Moon and planets are essential for choosing the correct gem. These angles vary as you move across the globe. Therefore, at each new location you would need a different gem recommendation.

Unfortunately, 99% of all astrologers today do not know this secret. When they make their recommendations you must be aware of the effect their gems will have on you! Even better, before a gem is recommended for you, ask for your horoscope to be reviewed based on your new place of residence.

Real Life Testimonial

30 carat lab-created ruby

A 56-year-old German business man moved to England based on a relocation reading. Even though his main chart (janma kundali) was the same, the Vedic astrology wealth chart (hora varga) was much better there. Within three months he signed the largest contract of his life. It was 50 times greater than any business he had done before. This man now lives a very easy life and recommends relocation to all his friends.

Quote

"But the totality had other plans and one morning I woke up with a realization. And the realization was: 'I need to move to the west coast of North America.' Didn't know why and so I moved. And then later, much later, I realized that I needed to be in that energy field for the book and the teaching to come out of me. And then it unfolded there."

Eckhart Tolle, in an audio entitled "Touching the Eternal" (Lecture 10, IndiaTrip, 2002)

Lab-created, 220 carat emerald

Secret 4 Summary

You need to be in the right place at the right time. And you need to wear a gem that fits your current place of residence, not your birthplace.

Secret 5

Effects of Gems on the Aura

The gem effect is not magic; we would rather call it the latest science. Our lives are governed by quantum energy fields much more than yesterday's science would want us to believe. Knowledge of these fields, their relationship to our bodies, mind and soul, and how they are entangled with the cosmic planetary quantum fields is the untold secret of selecting the proper gem. To do it properly requires an expert Vedic astrologer with years of training.

Traditionally, these quantum fields have been known as *auras*. They are energy fields surrounding the body. Very sensitive persons can see them with their eyes and describe them in various colors. A variety of measuring devices for the aura have also been developed. Some of them can picture the aura in a way similar to a photograph.

Gems filter white sunlight and enrich the aura with their specific colors. These colors are connected with the cosmic quantum fields of the Sun, Moon and planets. A gem, when properly selected from one's individual horoscope, including consideration of relocation, connects one's individual quantum fields to the cosmic quantum fields. This results in a balancing of the quantum fields, thereby warding off negative influences and strengthening the positive.

When the gem is large enough nearly everybody who wears or holds it can physically feel its vibrational influence. A sort of charging-up effect of the gem occurs over a period of several months. During this time the gem grows more and more efficient. The overall result then is an improved destiny for the wearer.

Real Life Testimonial

The authors of this book regularly test the immediate effects of gems on their clients. The client sits down, relaxed, with his/her hands open on the knees. The gem is then placed in one hand and the client gently grasps the stone with eyes closed. Within 2-3 minutes, nearly everybody has an experience of the gem's vibration emanating up the arms and around the whole body. Some have experiences of vibration in their various chakras, such as the forehead, heart and stomach. Some feel it in their spine. Others get tingles in their feet. Others feel warmth or coldness.

Lab-created white sapphire 29 carat

All these are the immediate effects as the gem re-aligns the individual quantum fields, enlivening the aura and every cell in the body. The intensity of these effects clearly increases with the size of the gem used. We have found from these experiences that the minimum gem size should be 24 carats.

Quote

Sri Yukteswar: "Mukunda (Yogananda's boyhood name), why don't you get an astrological armlet?"

Yogananda: "Should I, Master? I don't believe in astrology."

Sri Yukteswar: "It is never a question of belief; the only scientific attitude one can take on any subject is whether it is true. The law of gravitation worked as efficiently before Newton as after him. The cosmos would be fairly chaotic if its laws could not operate without the sanction of human belief."

From Paramahansa Yogananda, *Autobiography of a Yogi*, Chapter 16. "Outwitting the Stars".

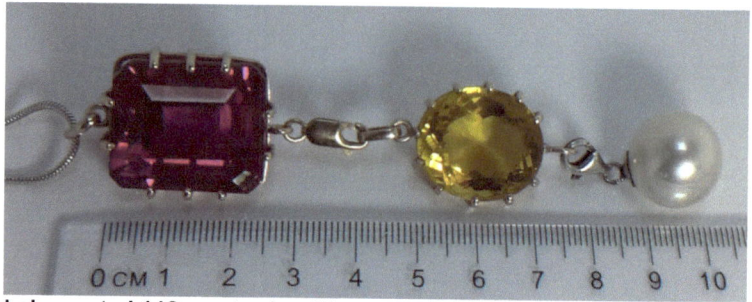

Lab-created 112 carat ruby, 35 carat yellow sapphire, 18mm pearl

Secret 5 Summary

Gems filter out certain frequencies from white sunlight. When correctly chosen, they improve the individual quantum fields known as auras and create a better destiny for the individual.

Secret 6

Gems for the Nine Planetary Quantum Fields

The following table connects the solar system dynamics of Sun, Moon, planets and lunar nodes (*Rahu* and *Ketu,* the ascending and descending intersection points of the Moon's orbit with the Ecliptic plane) with their respective jewels and their Sanskrit names:

Weekday	Jewel	Sanskrit	Trans-literated	Heavens	Rainbow
Sunday	Ruby	पद्मराग	padmarāga	Sun	Red
Monday	Pearl	मुक्ता	muktā	Moon	Orange
Tuesday	Red Coral	प्रवाल	pravāla	Mars	Yellow
Wednesday	Emerald	मरकत	marakata	Mercury	Green
Thursday	Yellow sapphire	पुष्पराग	puṣparāga	Jupiter	Blue
Friday	Diamond	वज्र	vajra	Venus	Indigo
Saturday	Blue sapphire	महानील	mahānīla	Saturn	Violet
	Hessonite	गोमेदक	gomedaka	Rahu	Ultra-Violet
	Cat's eye	वैदूर्य	vaidūrya	Ketu	Infra-red

Correct selection of gems should never be carried out according to birth month, or the Zodiac sign of the Sun. This has no significance for changing the quantum fields.

You must look at your individual birth chart to change your quantum fields and your aura and thus to improve your destiny. See Secret 3. Always use the relocated birth chart.

Real Life Testimonial

45 carat lab-created emerald

A well-situated 48-year-old English lady tried all sorts of birth stones and never experienced any real effect. She had a Jyotish gem consultation based on her individual birth chart. The recommendation was for an 18-carat emerald which she duly obtained.

Within two weeks she found that her creativity had improved substantially, so much so that she started to design jewelery for the first time. Her designs were totally stunning and beautiful. She created a new income source for herself and was very happy and fulfilled that she had found something very meaningful in her life.

Quote

"There are many types of jewels. Some of the more important ones are vajra (diamond), muktā (pearl), mani (ruby), padmarāga (ruby), marakata (emerald), indranīla (blue sapphire), vaidūrya (cat's eye), puṣparāga (topaz, yellow sapphire), karketana (chrysoberyl), pulaka (garnet), rudhira (carnelian), sphaṭika (quartz crystal) and pravāla (coral)."

Garuḍa Purāṇa, as told by Romaharshaṇa, a student of Veda Vyāsa, chapter on jewels.

Secret 6 Summary

You should obtain the correct set of gems based on your individual birth chart, relocated to your place of residence. The recommendation must be made by an experienced Vedic astrologer.

Secret 7

The Story of the Creation of Natural Gems

Geologists do not actually know how the various naturally-occurring precious gems have been created. They speculate that some types of gems have crystallized out from molten magma under the influence of high pressure and temperature. Yet, they cannot explain why gems occur only in certain deposits rather than being uniformly distributed over the Earth. Moreover, they are aware that these crystallization processes may not have taken millions of years. These processes may have occurred millions of years ago, but typically the gems are formed quite quickly – within a few weeks or months.

In lieu of a complete "scientific" explanation, it is interesting to note the ancient Vedic tradition on this subject which is found in the *Purāṇas*. It is the best explanation we have found so far, and it is reproduced in its entirety in Appendix 2, below:

According to this account, an ancient race of very advanced space travelers, called *devas,* saved the Earth from an event that threatened to extinguish all life on the planet. A gigantic asteroid, identified as the demon *Balāsura*, was on a path that would have lead to a direct impact on the surface of the planet. The *devas* attached the asteroid to their space ship in order to alter the asteroid's course before it moved around the Sun and hit the Earth.

The Earth was saved from the full impact of the asteroid, but the ship was moving too fast and the asteroid came loose, breaking up into several large pieces which crashed into the planet. The result was the creation of deposits of precious stones of different kinds owing, in each case, to the influence of different natural laws. According to the Purāṇas:

1. One fragment, moving close to the Sun, melted into fluid red magma, appearing like blood. It was then pushed out of orbit and impacted the Earth. Quickly cooling down in the evaporating waters of rivers, these fragments of the asteroid formed the origin of rubies.

2. Other fragments impacted on the oceans, forming tiny crystals like molten glass dropped into water. These sharp crystals can be seen in the oceans today and form the seeds for pearls in oysters.

3. Fragments that impacted on ocean shores and were cooled slowly by the waters of the nearby ocean were the origin of blue sapphires.

4. The sound of the impact of other fragments echoing from mountains created such intense pressure that it transformed crystal structures – the origin of cat's eye.

Secret 7 Summary

Natural gems, while having been created millions of years ago, actually took only a few weeks or months to form. The Vedic Puranas tell us the gems were created from fragments of an asteroid impact. See Appendix 2

Secret 8

Out of the Ground or From the Lab?

Gems from the ground are very expensive, due not merely to their intrinsic, material value but because they are so rare, especially when they are free of impurities and well colored.

A common myth holds that natural gem stones have been formed during millions of years in the womb of the Earth. But, in reality, it takes exactly the same amount of time (3 weeks to 6 months) and temperature (up to 3,500°C) to form a lab-created gem as it takes to form a gemstone in the Earth. The same laws of nature apply when crystals are grown in magma or, for example, from the impact of an asteroid. Even crystals within the magma do not take hundreds of years to form, although many stones from the ground may have been formed millions of years ago. It is simply a romantic conception of the jewelery industry that helps them sell expensive gems.

Any crystals that have the same geometric structure will resonate in the same way. It is the atomic lattice that influences and modifies any vibration or electromagnetic field, including visible light. As we read in Wikipedia (the entry on "Gemstone"): "... lab created gemstones are not imitations. For example, diamonds, rubies, sapphires and emeralds have been manufactured in labs to possess identical chemical and physical characteristics to the naturally occurring variety." The major difference between lab-created and natural gems is simply the higher purity of the former.

As lab-generated gems are created in a controlled, non-disturbed environment they have less inclusions (foreign crystal material), color zone changes, pressure fractures and other flaws. Due to their perfect symmetrical harmony, supporting coherent quantum fields, lab-grown crystals are more valuable for astrological purposes. They also have important industrial applications. Laser light is one example of this. A mined ruby would never create this highly orderly coherent light, and therefore cannot be used to manufacture lasers. Only lab gems support this highly orderly wave function.

Most astrologers know very little about gems because they are not trained gemologists. They have an incorrect viewpoint towards man-made gems, categorizing them all as "imitation" stones, disregarding the wide range of quality found in gems of this sort.

A good lab-grown gem (also called a "created gem") has exactly the same material, color and chemical composition as the natural gem, without the imperfections found in the "naturally" occurring stones. Our experience clearly shows that such gems have astrological "power". They change the destiny of the wearers, and do so very quickly in higher carat sizes like 50, 100 or even 200 carats. (See the various testimonials.) On the other hand, many gems of far lower quality are also artificially manufactured; we would call these the true "imitation" stones. While they can appear very similar, often with the same color, for example, these stones are made from different materials with different crystal lattices.

Only carefully selected, lab-created gems allow individuals to achieve fast improvements in their destiny at an affordable price. One does not have to spend gigantic amounts of money to obtain gems the size of crown jewels. Today, in our technological age, with fast travel by cars and airplanes, natural gems are as useful as donkeys pulling their little carts. Just keep feeding them 1 or 2 carats.

One further consideration is significant here -- the amount of suffering caused by the mining process of natural gems. Hundreds of thousands of poor people and even children have to labor in mines, sometimes under life threatening conditions. This is well documented in the 2006 movie *Blood Diamond* which is based on real conditions in the natural gem industry. Consider how much negative *karma* you have supported before trying to mitigate your own *karma* with a so-called "natural" gem! This, in itself, is a sufficient reason to prefer a laboratory-grown gem.

Some traditionalists and other superstitious people, in spite of a wealth of real life testimonials, still cannot be convinced of lab-created gems' astrological "power". The more scientific minded should analyze the following comparison chart of emeralds as an example. Measured variations in the chart occur in lab-created gems the same way as in natural gem deposits.

220 carat laboratory-grown emerald

Natural and Laboratory-Grown Emeralds Compared

Properties	Lab-Created Emeralds	Natural Emeralds
Chemical Composition	$Be_3Al_2(SiO_3)_6$ Beryllium aluminum silicate	$Be_3Al_2(SiO_3)_6$ Beryllium aluminum silicate
Crystallographic Character	Flattened hexagonal prismatic	Hexagonal prismatic habit
Refractive Index	1.570 - 1.576	1.564 - 1.595
Birefringence	0.005 - 0.006	0.005 - 0.007
Optical Character	Uni-axial	Uni-axial
Pleochroism	Green & bluish green	Green & bluish green
Dispersion	0.014	0.014
Hardness Mohs Scale	7.5 – 8.0	7.5 – 8.0
Toughness	Fair to poor, depending on quality	Fair to poor, depending on quality
Cleavage	Imperfect	Imperfect
Specific Gravity	Average 2.76	Average 2.76

Degree of Transparency	Transparent to translucent	Transparent to translucent
Transparency to X-Rays	Opaque	Opaque
X-Ray Fluorescence	None	None
Ultraviolet	Bright Red	Usually none, rarely distinct red
Color Filter Reaction	Bright Red	Bright Red, rarely none
Effect of Heat	Fuses with difficulty to a glass	Fuses with difficulty to a glass
Effect of Acid	Resists all but hydrofluoric	Resists all but hydrofluoric

Real Life Testimonial

"On 1 December 2000, the United Nations General Assembly adopted, unanimously, a resolution on the role of diamonds in fueling conflict, breaking the link between the illicit transaction of rough diamonds and armed conflict, as a contribution to prevention and settlement of conflicts (A/RES/55/56). In taking up this agenda item, the General Assembly recognized that conflict diamonds are a crucial factor in prolonging brutal wars in parts of Africa, and underscored that legitimate diamonds contribute to prosperity and development elsewhere on the continent.

"In Angola and Sierra Leone, conflict diamonds continue to fund the rebel groups, the National Union for the Total Independence of Angola (UNITA) and the Revolutionary United Front (RUF), both of which are acting in contravention

of the international community's objectives of restoring peace in the two countries.

"Rough diamond caches have often been used by rebel forces to finance arms purchases and other illegal activities. Neighboring and other countries can be used as trading and transit grounds for illicit diamonds. Once diamonds are brought to market, their origin is difficult to trace, and once polished, they can no longer be identified."

United Nations Resolution (A/RES/55/56) adopted by the General Assembly on "The Role of Diamonds in Fueling Conflict", 1st December, 2000. Was on the UN Website: http://www.un.org/peace/africa/Diamond.html Now here: books.google.co.uk/books?id=6IFoADVf4pIC&pg=PA149#

Quote

Maharishi Mahesh Yogi throughout his life took bold and practical steps to achieve world peace with the creation of "Invincibility for Every Nation" through large meditation groups.

Maharishi accepted the positive effects of lab-created gems as long as they are very close to the original. He inspired scientists to examine them from a scientific viewpoint. Here is a quote from an audio recording made on 2nd February, 1969, in Rishikesh, India:

"Question: There are certain stones that men could make in laboratories now, like sapphires and diamonds and emeralds and things like that. Is man helping out somehow in the evolution of rock, the evolution of matter? Do they have a different significance to the ones you find in the rocks, in the caves?"

Maharishi: "Depending on how near the truth is the imitation. (Laughs) How near the truth is the copy. So we can adopt." Questioner: "They are completely the same molecules."

Maharishi: *"Molecules are the same; electrons may be different. Hmmm. Same molecules?"*

Questioner: *"They can make them identical to the original now."*

Maharishi: *"Very good. Deeper the knowledge of the basic things, more is the possibilities on these expressed values."*

Secret 8 Summary

Gems grown properly in the lab are cheaper, far superior for astrology, available in larger sizes and larger quantities, and they do not cause any suffering or hardship for the workers in natural gem mines.

Lab-created yellow sapphire 42 carat

Secret 9

Avoid Treated Natural Gems

Driven by the increasingly lucrative jewel market, the natural gem industry has many dark secrets to hide. Since the beginning of the new millennium, for example, gems are increasingly being treated to make them appear more valuable.

Today 99.9% of rubies in the market are heat-treated. A large proportion of red or pink mined rubies have flaws – purple and black spots and other color variations. Through the process of heating them to nearly melting temperature these flaws disappear. But the result is that the crystal structure of the ruby is destroyed. This effectively converts the ruby crystal into glass at those flawed spots. Heating dissolves the molecular crystal lattice which is so important in creating the quantum field effect. Basically, therefore, a heat-treated ruby in its qualities is more like red colored glass. It may look pretty, but has no astrological effect.

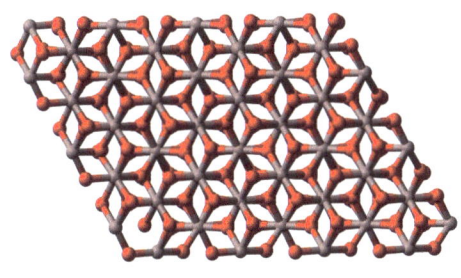

Corundum crystal lattice. Photo © public domain from Wikipedia

This is the orderly crystal lattice of corundum Al_2O_3. Aluminum and oxygen atoms form regular patterns. Rubies and sapphires of any color are basically corundum.

Heat-treated rubies and sapphires, on the other hand, are similar to glass. It is really cheating to call these items "rubies". One could save a lot of money by buying red glass instead of heat-treated "rubies".

The amorphous structure of glass, on the right, is more like a fluid than a regular crystal. Heat-treatment of gems close to their melting temperature usually creates such disorderly structures.

The same story applies to all varieties of colored corundum, such as blue and yellow sapphire. Honest gem wholesalers will tell you that today 97% of all blue sapphires are heat-treated to intensify or deepen the color, and to amalgamate any inclusions. Most yellow sapphires on the market are heat-treated as well. But color created by heat-treating often fades within a year or two.

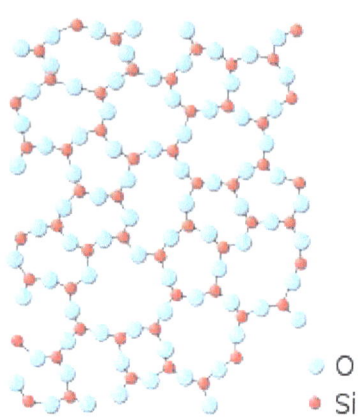

Amorphous structure of glass silica. Photo © public domain from Wikipedia

○ O
● Si

Green natural emeralds are subject to some of the worst manipulation. Most of them are fracture-filled with plastic resin or green oil with the same refractive index. The fractures are vacuum acid-cleaned and then heat-treated and oiled. The whole process is designed to enhance their appearance and justify their high prices. Actually, it only disguises the heavy flaws of those natural gems and completely disrupts their orderly crystal structure. We would call these processes deceitful.

Also, most red coral is dyed. The basic material can be white coral, bone, ceramics, or glass beads. These dyes actually leach out into clothes and skin. Of course, they have no effect on your aura and destiny.

If you wish to avoid all those traps, emptying your pockets without delivering any value, it is best to go for lab-created gems from the beginning. They are designed to have a proper crystal lattice. The best quality of rubies we use can even support laser light function. This happens only when the crystal lattice is perfect.

Real Life Testimonial

A 42-year-old English business man spent £6,000 on a 4-carat emerald and felt no effects. He later found out from another jeweler that this gem had been heat-treated and injected with oil. Then he purchased a second 5-carat natural emerald for £8,000. This still had no effect.

Fed up with all these manipulations, he became our client and purchased a 36-carat lab-created emerald (neither heat-treated, nor oiled). He donated £4,000 towards our research efforts. His business soared like an eagle. He became one of the richest men in his community.

Quote

"A sapphire should never be flung into a fire. The person who does this deed suffers great misfortune."

Garuḍa Purāṇa as told by Romaharshaṇa, a student of Veda Vyāsa, chapter on jewels

Secret 9 Summary

Natural gems are increasingly subject to processing, such as being heat-treated and oiled, and as a result have no astrological benefits. Since 99% of natural gems on the market today have these created faults, it is simpler and cheaper to buy a good lab-created gem with a correct crystal structure.

Secret 10

How to Fulfill Your Desires

There are gems that have a good effect on your destiny and others that have a bad effect. Obviously, everyone prefers good effects. Most horoscopes suggest the choice of two, three, or even four positive gems.

Gems are not just for general well-being but can also be specific to your wishes and desired destiny. By making the right choice you can influence the changes in your destiny. Here free will comes in again. For example, you can choose to have an increase in wealth as a first priority, improved happiness as second priority and improved health as third priority. These priorities should be told to your Vedic astrologer before he chooses the proper gem for you.

In case you cannot afford several gems immediately, we found it to be a very intelligent route to choose increased wealth first. This will put you in a position to acquire more and larger gems to increase your wealth further, and to have all the other positive effects in your life. See Secret 14 for more details.

Even if you call yourself a very spiritual person, be practical and put yourself into a situation where you can afford all those positive effects of many gems. This will include increased spiritual experiences as well.

We want to give you an idea on the pricing of large, inclusion-free natural gems. At the time of writing this book there were two offers from Thailand for large yellow sapphires on Ebay. One of them was a 101-carat yellow-golden natural sapphire offered for sale at $19 million (£12 million). The other one was also a yellow sapphire, this one of 104 carats, offered at $12 million (£7.6 million). Of course both of them are very rare, highest quality gems. They are totally free of inclusions.

We are well aware that most of our readers cannot afford such expensive natural gems. Therefore it is interesting to note that we believe the same astrological effect can be created from lab-created gems with a similar clarity and totally inclusion-free. These generally cost less than 0.1% of the price of the large natural gems that have been offered on Ebay. With lab-created gems you can afford to get the power of the crown jewels without having to pay a king's ransom.

Real Life Testimonial

During her brief career, a 47-year-old English mother and property speculator had acquired three of her own houses. Before the end of her career she wanted to own five houses altogether. This would give her one house for each of her four children, and one of her own.

We analyzed her horoscope for the specific purpose of determining how she could acquire more property. We recommended a 22-carat, lab-created yellow sapphire. She purchased it but did not give us much immediate feedback. On meeting her a year later, the first question we asked her: "How many houses do you own now?" To our surprise she answered, "17! Yes, I own 17 houses now, and now I understand why you had told me a year ago that I needed to work only for another year. I decided to take early retirement."

Quote

"A hymn accompanying investiture with an amulet of gold:

"Gold that was born from Fire is immortal, has been deposited with mortal creatures. He who knows this deserves to own this jewel, and in extreme old age dies he who wears it.

"The men of ancient times, with children round them, longed for this gold, bright with the Sun's own color. This shall endow thee as it shines with splendor, and long shall be the life of him who wears it.

"Long life and splendor, let it bring energy and strength to thee. That thou mayst shine among the folk with all the brightness of the gold."

Atharva Veda, 19.26.1 – 3, translation by Ralph T.H. Griffith, 1895

White lab-sapphire, 29 carats

Yellow lab-sapphire, 42 carats

Secret 10 Summary

Be the master of your own destiny. Fulfil all your desires with the proper gems.

Secret 11

Selection Method: Strengthen Positive, Not Negative

Do not fight the darkness – increase the light! Research performed by Richard S. Brown on 5,000 people (see the Real Life Testimonial below) has shown that it is by far the best approach to strengthen positive traits by selecting the right gem for your functionally positive planets.

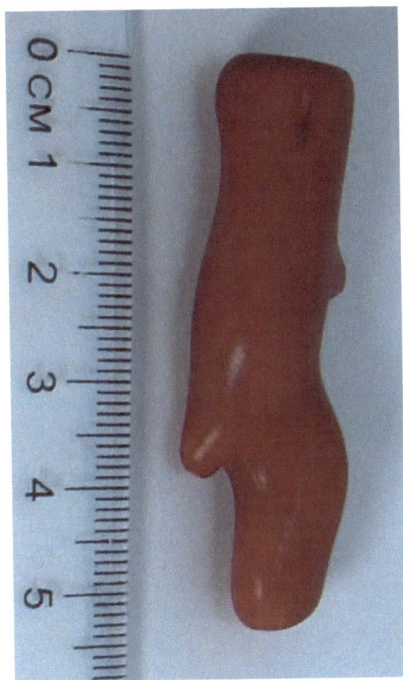

81 carat red coral for Mars

Many believe that a gem always increases the power of the heavenly body with which it is associated. But this is not quite true. In fact, the quantum field of the heavenly body is not changed at all. What is changed by the gem is the way in which the individual's quantum field interacts with the quantum field generated by the heavenly body. That interaction can be positive or negative, and a good Vedic astrologer or *Jyotishi* would see it in an individual horoscope. Only the positive interactions should be strengthened by wearing the correct gems. (See the planet and gem table in Secret 6.)

The oldest astrology scriptures, such as the *Brihat Pārāshara Horā Shāstra*, have a clear formula for calculating the power of a heavenly body, including the Sun, Moon, planets and lunar nodes. These are called *graha*s in Sanskrit. The power calculation – *bala* in Sanskrit – depends upon positions, angles, etc., but one term of the calculation describes the natural power exchange between the heavenly body's quantum field and the quantum field of the individual. This power factor can be increased by wearing a gem.

Arising from the increased power influence of a heavenly body, or *graha*, the whole individual horoscope shifts due to the altered planetary strength. The positive effects from a beneficial *graha* increase when the person wears the correct gem. This will effectively alter his/her horoscope and consequently his/her destiny.

Real Life Testimonial

"CONCLUSION (Harness the pure power of your lucky stars)

"My conclusions are based on Vedic scripture, common sense, and a 25 year study of over 5,000 persons using gems for their strong or good planets, as well as others using gems for their bad or weak planets. Gems related to good planets produced good results, while gems for bad planets produced BAD results.

"I think that some of today's Kali-Yuga (dark age) astrologers are doing a great disservice to the public by prescribing gems for BAD planets, and also telling people that it is OK to use FLAWED gems, in complete contradiction of the Shastras (Vedic scriptures).

"If it is true that bad planetary gems can harm a person, and flawed gems are actually inauspicious, then those who

recommend such inferior quality of stones are guilty of inflicting harm on fellow human beings."

Richard S. Brown, GIA, PG, Founding member of the Planetary Gemologists Association, in his article "Standardization of the Vedic Science of Planetary Gemmology", 26th April, 1999.

Quote

"The Jyotish gems act the SAME as their grahas (planets), and so the gems should be used for a native's ANUKUL GRAHAS (benefic planets) to harness the benefic influence. The Jyotish gems do not act OPPOSITE of their grahas and so gems should not be used for a native's PRATIKUL GRAHAS (malefic planets). Thus the malpractice of Pratikul Vad by some confused and irrational astrologers to the detriment even ruination of their misguided clients can be put to an end."

Pt. Pemmaraju V.R. Rayudu

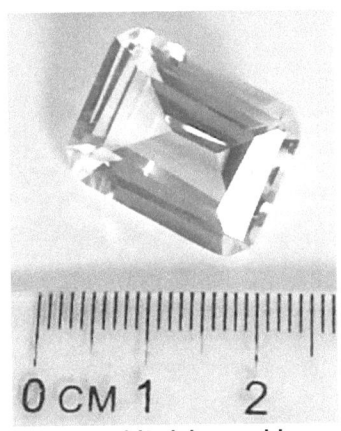

29 carat white lab-sapphire

Secret 11 Summary

Strengthen positive heavenly influences by wearing the gems for functionally positive planets in your birth chart, relocated to your place of residence.

Secret 12

Gem Combinations

Some individual's horoscopes allow only one good gem to be worn, others two, three or even four. If you are able to wear several gems you have a choice regarding what you wish to achieve with them. A good Vedic astrologer should be able to tell you the specific effects of each gem, as well as its possible side effects. By choosing the right gem or gem combinations you can fulfill specific desires that are important to you in your life.

Make sure that you tell those specific wishes to your Vedic astrologer before he chooses the right gem for you. Unfortunately, too many astrologers choose gems from a very superficial perspective, such as, for example, the 1-5-9 method. Talk with your Vedic astrologer about the method that he uses, and do not accept superficial recommendations. This is an additional rule to the fundamental selection method of Secret 11: *Strengthen Positive, Not Negative*.

If you have moved away from your birth place, you should also take care that your astrologer uses only the relocated chart. (See Secret 4.) If you miss that point, you may create a lot of wealth, health and happiness for an imaginary person who does not live there any more. You have to create the effect at the place where you are. This means that the gem selection must be based on your relocated chart. Unfortunately, 99% of all Vedic astrologers have neither heard of this nor studied the original literature in Sanskrit. The sage Parāshara knew this relocation secret, but most of his followers today use incorrect translations.

3 gem combination

From our clients, we have observed that gems work differently when they move around the planet. So, now we recommend specific combinations of gems depending on where they are located. This means that you will need to take off some of your gems when you go on a holiday. All of this can be accurately calculated.

Another very important aspect of wearing several gems are possible clashes between the various quantum fields of the gems. These clashes would clearly show up as physical tensions such as headaches and all sorts of unlucky strokes of destiny.

This too can be calculated in advance, and a good gem recommendation would tell you what gems should not be worn with other gems. It is all based on the "friendship" between the *grahas*, i.e. the Sun, Moon, planets and lunar nodes. This friendship depends on relative angles of the *grahas* in your native horoscope. The *graha* friendships stay constant even when moving around the globe. There is a general friendship matrix between each *graha* and each other *graha*, and also an individual friendship matrix, specific to the individual's horoscope. Make sure that your astrologer uses this individual friendship matrix only.

Real Life Testimonial

A US family with South Asian origins equipped themselves completely with gems, including the two parents, who were both medical doctors, and their two children. Each one of them obtained several gems which were chosen specifically, considering their individual horoscopes and their most cherished desires.

They all noticed immediate effects. The mother received several pay increases, and after about two years was offered one of the highest government jobs in their state. The father was gradually afforded more and more respect by his colleagues, enjoyed great new scientific insights from his research, and became a world renowned authority in his field of medicine.

In addition, the children started to do really well in school. The girl got rid of a painful skin disease and consequently developed higher self esteem. After wearing the gems for about four years, she was able to skip over one grade in school. The boy, who was not sure about his career before wearing his "lucky gems" as he called them, is now applying for medical school. He has become famous in his own town; even the mayor started to talk to this 18-year-old about some of the town's projects. It was all over the newspapers. You can be sure that his parents were extremely proud.

Quote

"That we find a crystal or a poppy beautiful means that we are less alone, that we are more deeply inserted into existence than the course of a single life would lead us to believe."

John Berger, British author

Secret 12 Summary

Use gem combinations to fulfill specific desires. Make sure that your astrologer considers all side effects, including relocation and planetary friendships, based on your horoscope.

Secret 13

The Square Law: Size Does Matter

Physicists have discovered a square law in many areas involving fields. For example, the achieved power is the square of the amplitude. This applies to all sorts of quantum fields, including light, or the power of sound developed by a loud speaker.

The experiences of gem wearers demonstrate this square law. What does it mean in practice?

It means that a gem has four times the effect of one half its size. With triple the size it has nine times the effect. In practical terms, this effect is revealed in the speed with which a gem brings about positive changes in someone's destiny. A 24-carat ruby, for example, is 12 times larger in volume than a 2-carat ruby, therefore the effect is 12 x 12 = 144 times. That means any positive effect that the 24-carat ruby would bring in 3 days would take more than a year with the 2-carat ruby.

Because of this square law, therefore, we recommend to our clients that they obtain the largest possible gems they can afford. You can physically experience the vibration of a large gem when placed in your hand. Larger gems improve your destiny much more quickly.

Many Indian and other Asian astrologers recommend specific gem sizes in terms of *ratti*, which is an old measure of weight. They believe that certain *ratti* sizes bring good luck and other sizes bring bad luck. We believe this is pure superstition. The laws of physics tell us: the larger, the better.

Real Life Testimonial

A highly spiritual, 60-year-old British man knew from his astrologer that a cat's eye gem would activate all previously acquired good karma. He started with a "small" 60-carat lab-created gem which manifested all sorts of business benefits. A year later, he obtained another cat's eye with a weight of 180 carats. This did the trick immediately. Within a month he signed the largest contract of his life, increasing his income by a factor of 100, and bringing him a completely new life style.

Quote

"And, Bold One, bring in ample store, rich jewels to adorn the ears, for thou, Good Lord, art far renowned."

Rig Veda 8.78.3, translation by Ralph T.H. Griffith, 1895

220 carat lab-created emerald

Secret 13 Summary

The larger the gems, the quicker the effects, sometimes occuring within days rather than years.

Secret 14

Increase the Size Over Time

From our experience with clients we have learned something very simple and practical. You will love this one! As the large lab-created gems create effects very quickly, the simplest way to afford many gems is as follows:

First, get hold of a gem that you can afford and which has the specific effect of bringing you more money. This "starter gem" will very quickly improve your financial situation and then you can afford to buy the same gem in larger sizes to create much more wealth. The minimum "starter gem" size should be 24 carats.

Based on your larger wealth you can now afford all the other gems, those that make you happy, healthy, improve family life, spirituality, etc. We found this to be a very practical and enjoyable sequence. It is far more practical to own ample wealth so that you can buy your most spiritually active gem, rather than long for it for the whole of your life, while you sit and meditate in poverty.

Real Life Testimonial

A young English entrepreneur of Indian origin found some good ways of earning money on the internet. He purchased a 36-carat emerald and within days his business really took off. His earnings multiplied many times. Three months later he obtained another lab-created emerald of 208 carats. According to the square law this has 33 times the effect of the smaller gem.

Lab-created emeralds 220 carat + 45 carat

Now everything in his life moved forward very quickly. He started to host large international conferences and was invited to the most prestigious events world-wide. A few weeks later, he and his family moved out from their small two-bedroom suburban house into a stately mansion with three floors, a large park, and two swimming pools, located at the best address in his city.

Quote

"Big girls need big diamonds."

Elizabeth Taylor, English-American actress

29 carat white lab-sapphire

Authors' comment: Diamonds are hard to produce in the labs beyond 5 carats and even those are very expensive. We have found that large lab-created white sapphires have similar destiny-improving qualities to diamonds. These can be produced at a reasonable cost in labs, with sizes up to 200 carats.

Secret 14 Summary

Large gems are very powerful. Therefore, it is wise to increase the size gradually to allow the body to adjust to the increased influence. Do not worry about the costs. The gems will bring the money.

Secret 15

Do Not Have it Too Big

We have found an upper limit for large gems. At around 200 carats the effects of the gems become so intensive that most owners cannot handle them. These over-sized gems can change their owner's destiny in unforeseen ways which are not practical while living on this planet.

In this context, also make sure you do not increase the gem size too quickly. Allow your physiology to adapt to the aura changes gradually. Generally, individuals with a heavier body type can handle larger stones more easily. Slim people should increase their gem sizes in smaller steps.

Real Life Testimonial

Here is the story of a very embarrassed, rich client from the UK. 600 carats of emerald is definitely toooooo much! First he purchased a 200-carat gem. Impressed with its brilliance he obtained another 200 carats. Life started to get really amazing. But this man was very greedy; he tested another 200-carat gem.

Here is what happened. He wanted to sign an official document. For that he had to travel 150 miles on the motorway network with his passport and other documents. First he wore the gems around his neck. He then found this was too intense, so he put them in the pockets of some trousers at the back of his 7-seater people-carrier.

Now these gems wanted to have fun! The rear door of the vehicle magically opened. A gust of wind took the trousers, the passport, the wallet and 600 carats of precious lab-created emeralds for a flight across the motorway.

When he returned to search for his treasure everything had disappeared completely. After hours of searching, he ended up at the local police station reporting the loss of his passport and driving license. He did not dare to mention the gems. Definitely, his destiny had changed within minutes. It took another month to get a new passport and driving license. He did bring some good luck to his gem supplier, however. He ordered another emerald, although this one was a mere 200 carats! But he was happy thereafter.

Quote

"May Earth, the Goddess, she who bears her treasure stored up in many a place, gold, gems and riches, giver of opulence, grant great possessions to us bestowing them with love and favor.

"Earth, bearing folk of many a varied language with diverse rites as suits their dwelling-places, pour like a constant cow that never faileth, a thousand streams of treasure to enrich me!"

Atharva Veda,12.1.44 and 45, translation by Ralph T.H. Griffith, 1895

Secret 15 Summary

The upper limit for large gems is 200 carats.

Secret 16

How to Wear Gems

Gems are most effective when worn correctly. The goal is to optimize the interaction between the cosmic and individual quantum fields. For this to occur, the light of the Sun, representing totality, has to shine through the gem onto your skin, except in the case of red coral and pearl, where the light is reflected from the gem.

The gem has to be set correctly. The metal setting of the gem should be minimum, and the visible area of the gem, both front and back, should be as great as possible. In this way you maximize the sunlight that can shine through, or reflect from, the gem and improve your aura, and thus your destiny.

Ask your astrologer what would be the best metal for the gem setting. For some charts this is gold, for others silver or other precious metals.

Also, it is a great advantage to wear clothes that maximize the amount of sunlight penetrating or reflecting from the gem. When you wear dark colors you reduce the sunlight. Wearing light colors, and colors similar to the gem, brings the best benefit.

The minimum size of a gem we ever recommend to our clients is 24 carats. All of them, without exception, have experienced immediate improvements in their lives. With smaller gems this does not happen so quickly; some improvements could take a whole life time to occur. Be happy and keep feeding your donkey 1 or 2 carats for a whole life time!

Flexible pendant setting of large lab-gems

OK, now back to the big boys and girls. You can wear large gems either on a pendant or an arm bangle. It would be impractical to wear them on a finger.

You should never let anyone touch your gemstone as you run the risk of introducing foreign and unwanted frequencies into it. This will negatively affect any benefit to you.

Real Life Testimonial

One of our clients has developed a flexible pendant setting for several gems. Each gem is attached by a single ring or a clasp to the gem above. This string of gems can actually be extended. One special advantage of this particular setting: the gems do not clash together and do not create scratch marks.

Quote

"As God delights in his own beauty, he must necessarily delight in the creature's holiness which is a conformity to and participation of it, as truly as brightness of a jewel, held in the Sun's beams, is a participation or derivation of the Sun's brightness, though immensely less in degree."

Jonathan Edwards (1703-1758, theologian, philosopher of British American Puritanism, stimulator of the religious revival "Great Awakening")

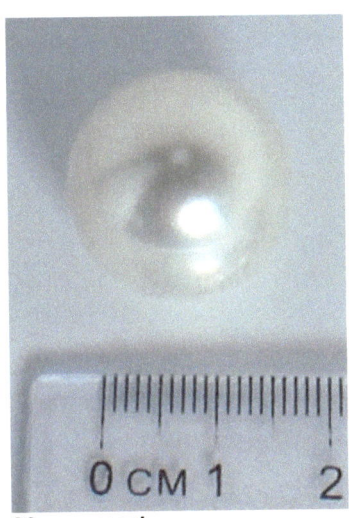

20 mm pearl

Secret 16 Summary

Wear the gem so that you maximize the sunlight shining through it, or, in the case of red coral and pearl, reflecting from it. The effect is created from the filtered sunlight touching your skin.

Secret 17

When to Wear Gems

There are astrological phases in your life, called *dasha*s in Sanskrit. These phases outline the auspicious and inauspicious periods in your life. Each phase is associated with a *graha* (Sun, Moon, planets, lunar nodes) and brings back that part of your destiny which is connected to the *graha*.

For example, in the Jupiter *dasha* all those elements of your destiny connected to Jupiter are brought to you. When these elements are good and favorable, it is advisable to wear the gem yellow sapphire for Jupiter in that life period.

One interesting point about these gems: as they are so large, their power can be focused by holding them in the hand. In this way they have a very special effect on your actions. You are literally holding your destiny in your own hand. Use your power!

Normally, you wear your gems during the light hours of the day. At night you can take them off. Remember, their power unfolds under light.

From time to time it is good to cleanse your gems. You can do that by holding them under running cold water, or by placing them in water or organic milk on the window sill, so that the light waves from the Sun and Moon cleanse them.

Real Life Testimonial

A 24-year-old English lady wanted to get married to her boy friend whom she had known for the past five years. He bought her a 150-carat lab-created cat's eye. For some reason, her mother did not reveal the lady's correct birth time at first. Based on that incorrect information, her Vedic astrologer prescribed the cat's eye to reduce general fear, etc.

Within four months, her friend, who was a millionaire by then (he also wore large gems), made up his mind and agreed to the marriage. The parents got involved in organizing their wedding, at which time the mother found the lady's correct birth time.

Now the astrologer recast the horoscope with the correct birth time and found that it had changed. In her correct horoscope the effect of the cat's eye was not to reduce fear, but to attract a good partner. This worked out wonderfully, and three months later they were a happily married couple.

Quote

"These gems have life in them: their colors speak, say what words fail of."

George Eliot, English novelist

Secret 17 Summary

Wear the gems effectively in sunlight hours, and amplify their power when needed by holding them in your hands.

Secret 18

Relief of Not Wearing the Wrong Gems or Metals

48 carat blue lab-sapphire

Every horoscope has a house of loss. It is the last one of the twelve houses. There are also some other unfortunate houses. The *grahas* (Sun, Moon, planets, lunar nodes) connected to these houses bring about loss and negative experiences. Therefore it is unwise to increase such negative influences.

When someone wears the wrong gems or metals they actually increase bad luck. To get rid of the bad luck, simply remove those gems or metals. This is secret 18.

Real Life Testimonial

One of our first clients, many years ago, was a 55-year-old woman who loved gold jewelery. When we met her she was in an extended period of bad luck. She had a minor car accident with no injuries to anyone, just car damage. Police were called and for some reason (call it destiny) she was very aggressive towards them. She was taken to the police station and locked up for the first time in her life. She was then subsequently bailed out, to appear in court some time later.

After calling us for help, we arranged to meet her. She told her whole deplorable story and also told us of some other negative events. For example, the day before, she had lost her watch. The morning of the same day her washing machine broke down. Her landlord threatened to cancel her rental agreement. This lady was in a real mess!

We told her not to worry and checked the horoscope. There we found that gold was not good for her. As she was wearing several gold necklaces, rings, broaches and bangles, we suggested that she removed them immediately to escape the bad luck. She did it reluctantly and also ordered a yellow sapphire that would bring her good luck instead.

We met her a second time just before her court case to hand her the 17-carat yellow sapphire. Again she still had some golden jewelery on. We told her that the bad luck would continue with the gold. Now she got the message and removed gold for good. She even refrained from wearing gold-colored shoes.

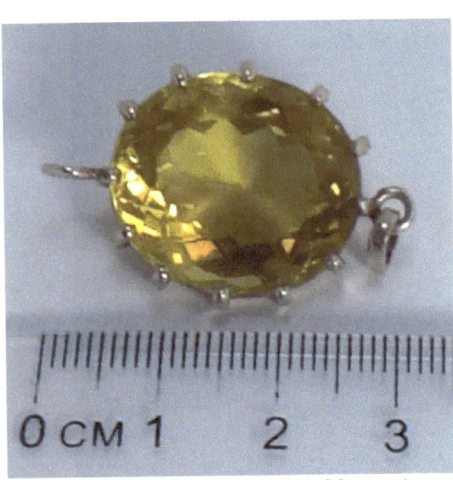

Lab-created yellow sapphire 36 carat

From that time everything went positively for her. Her case came up in court the next day and she was completely exonerated. Her lawyer told her she could now sue the police for £15,000 for wrongful arrest. Next, she found the lost watch and had the washing machine repaired. A week later her landlord renewed her rental contract.

The influence of <u>not</u> wearing some metal or gems can also change your destiny very quickly.

Quote

*"My crown is in my heart, not in my head,
Nor decked with diamonds and Indian stones,
Nor to be seen; my crown is called contentment;
A crown it is, that seldom kings enjoy."*

William Shakespeare from "King Henry the Sixth", Act 3, Scene 1

Secret 18 Summary

Do not wear gems or metals that bring you bad luck.

Secret 19

Increase Your Consciousness

It is possible to escape the influence of your horoscope. This is called enlightenment. It is a state of total freedom. Destiny, whether good or bad, no longer reaches you. Sun and Moon and all the planets will be favourable and support whatever you want to achieve in the moment.

To all those who place their attention on enlightenment: Enlightened sages throughout history have declared that *There is no path to enlightenment.* All there is is a pathless path. That means all you have to achieve is to realize it for yourself. You cannot learn how to become enlightened, you can only be it.

Start living in the moment and fulfill your desires rather than anyone else's. Get yourself an astro gem. This will help you change your aspirations and create a sustainable, positive environment around yourself.

To sustain these effects, the only thing left to do is to learn to meditate. You can then start to realize, and be able to use, the amazing powers bestowed upon you by the increased coherence of your mind and body living in perfect harmony.

The wise of all ages have recommended spiritual practise to achieve enlightenment. Wearing large gems can create a comfortable situation so that you may realize enlightenment, but it is not sufficient. You should do some regular practise such as meditation, breathing exercises and yoga, for example.

From our own experience we can confirm to you that enlightenment exists and it can be achieved immediately, in a very easy way. Start living in the moment!

Real Life Testimonial

There are stages of enlightenment and the highest is called unity consciousness. In this state all the worlds are experienced as oneness and so-called supernatural experiences – in Sanskrit, Sidhis – become a natural part of daily living. Such an enlightened one gave this report:

"My Sidhi techniques create the experience whenever I practise them. Each one. Always. Immediately. Even during normal daytime activities Sidhi experiences come about spontaneaously. Daily life with Sidhis is absolutely amazing: be it a bird or a dog whose speach I can spontaneously understand, the experience of stars and planets, the sight of past and future, the vision inside of the body with all its organs, or finding any knowledge through inner light. These experiences have now become a day-to-day reality and I have experienced them in thousands of variations. They have totally changed my life and my vision of what the world is.

"The day is full of joy and happiness and my environment notices this: be it the little doggies who run away from their owners only to walk a bit of the way with me and my friends; be it the small children who feel magically attracted by the happiness that they experience while playing in my vicinity; be it the many people who momentarily loose their memory and simply cannot remember their previous worries. Life is Bliss!"

Another enlightened one gave his report:

"Here are some expressions of living in perfect harmony. Having dreamed about being invisible, I have now been able to fulfill this as I have found a way of deflecting the light from

another's eyes. This is one of the Sidhis of Patañjali. I usually notice this as I walk through the local supermarket. My friends can walk by me without recognizing me.

"There are no longer coincidences in my life, just the fulfillment of all my desires. Innocent desires get fulfilled within 24 hours and sometimes immediately. Some of my older desires have now been fulfilled. I am rich beyond my dreams and everyday it increases without work. Daily life is just a playground. I am now getting bliss within bliss. Every day is just one long laugh.

"Using Patañjali's Sidhi techniques I am able to visit objects on the microscopic level. I look at atoms everyday, their construction and the electron fog around them. Speaking with physicists, I have confirmed my observations far beyond their present day knowledge. They were amazed about the amount of details I could tell them, which no one had researched before.

"It is the same story in traveling through the universes using my enlightened mind. It is so much fun. Having the ability to travel from one galaxy to the next, I perceive planets, colors, gas clouds and the vast, dark space. I actually pause to watch all these cosmic events happen. At times, I perceive my consciousness expanded to the farthest extent of the universe. At the same time, I can still focus the attention to any point in the universe and can hear speech and can see peoples living in far distant places and other universes.

"These are the domains of an enlightened individual living on Planet Earth today. Why not come and join us with much love."

Quote

"Do not base your life on the likings and dis-likings or whims of others. What you are in life – whether you enjoy or suffer – it is your own responsibility. Be regular in your meditation and do not postpone for a later date your striving for God consciousness."

Maharishi Mahesh Yogi

Secret 19 Summary

You have now arrived at Gate 19. This is your portal to Heaven on Earth! Your ticket will be checked shortly.

Contact

Authors

Contact the authors via e-mail:

Dr. Heinz Krug   drheinz@birthtime.info

Dr. Robert Thurston   vediccrystal@gmx.co.uk

Website

News and links to buy the eBook or paperback:

http://astrogembook.com

To get specific gem information e-mail:
info@astrogembook.com

Appendix 1

Weight Measures

1 carat	= 0.2 gram	
1 ratti	= 0.12125 gram	
1 tola	= 12 masha	= 11.67 gram
1 masha	= 8 ratti	= 0.97 gram

Appendix 2

Cited below, the complete chapter on jewels from the *Garuḍa Purāṇa* as told by Romaharshaṇa, a student of Veda Vyāsa:

Jewels

"A long time ago, there was a demon named Balāsura. He defeated Indra and the other gods. Balāsura was invincible. Not knowing what to do, the gods arranged a yajna. They then went to Balāsura and asked him for his body so that it might be offered as a sacrifice at the yajna. The demon was generous and he was not going to refuse a request, so he gave his body to the gods.

"The gods ascended a vimāna (space vehicle) and were traveling through the sky with Balāsura's body. But the vimāna was moving so fast that Balāsura's body fell off. It broke into many parts which got scattered throughout the Earth. Wherever a part of the body fell, earth, mountain or garden, that place became a source of jewels and precious stones.

"There are many types of jewels. Some of the more important ones are vajra (diamond), muktā (pearl), mani (ruby), padmarāga (ruby), marakata (emerald), indranīla (blue sapphire), vaidūrya (cat's eye), puṣparāga (topaz, yellow sapphire), karketana (chrysoberyl), pulaka (garnet), rudhira (carnelian), sphaṭika (quartz crystal) and pravāla (coral).

"Vajra or hīraka was formed from Balāsura's bones. Diamonds can be of many colors, coppery, milky-white, blue, golden, yellow and dark. Red and yellow diamonds should be worn only by a king, not by anyone else. A multicolored and round diamond should not be worn indiscriminately. It can cause great suffering, and due precautions have to be taken before such a diamond is worn as adornment. Even Indra takes care before wearing such a diamond. A hexagonal diamond is extremely rare and brings good fortune. A diamond is valuable because it can cut and mark any other object. But a diamond cannot be cut or marked except by another diamond.

"Muktas (pearls) can be obtained from eight different places, from elephants, clouds, boars, conch-shells, fish, snakes, oysters and bamboo, but oysters are the most common source. Pearls got from bamboo, elephants, fish, conch-shells and boars are not at all bright. Balāsura's teeth fell into the ocean. There the teeth entered the bodies of oysters and became the seeds for pearls. A pearl which weighs half a tola (weight) is worth 1305 coins. There are several other grades for pearls, the worth being 800, 783, 325, 200, 110, 100, 97, 40, 30, 14, 11 and 9 coins respectively. If you need to polish a pearl, put it inside the stomach of a fish. Cover the fish with clay and roast it. The pearl should then be taken out and washed with milk, wine and water. It will become bright and shining. What happens if one suspects that a pearl is not genuine? It should be kept in saline water for a night and then dried. If its color does not fade, it is a genuine pearl.

"Balāsura's blood fell into a river. In fact, at first it had not fallen into the river at all, but was retained by the Sun. But Rāvaṇa, king of Lanka, once decided to attack the Sun. And in the process, the Sun dropped Balāsura's blood into a river which came to be known as Rāvaṇagaṅgā. This blood became rubies (padmarāga). Rubies are red. Some of them may be tinged with a little bit of black or blue. A good quality ruby should never be worn with a bad quality ruby. The wearer of a good quality ruby is protected from all misfortunes.

"The king of the snakes is Vāsuki. Vāsuki accepted the bile (pitta) that came out of Balāsura's body. The snake was traversing the sky when he was suddenly attacked by

Garuḍa. Garuḍa too wanted to possess the bile. While the two were fighting, the bile fell into the valley of a mountain. This bile gave birth to marakatas (emeralds). Emeralds are generally green in color. The herbs which grow in emerald mines are cures for sorts of poison. A true emerald never fades in color.

"Balāsura's eyes fell on the shores of the ocean. And these eyes became indranīla jewels (sapphires). Sapphires are tinged with blue. A sapphire should never be flung into a fire. The person who does this deed suffers great misfortune. A special sort of sapphire is known as mahānīla. It is dark blue in color and if it is kept immersed in milk, the milk turns blue in color.

"Balāsura roared before he died. This roar echoed in a mountain range named Vidura. And from the roar was born a gem known as vaidūrya (cat's eye), so called because it can be found on the mountain Vidura. Vaidūryas are green or blue in color.

"Balāsura's skin fell on the Himalayas. This skin was the origin of puṣparāga (yellow sapphire). A puṣparāga is light yellow in color. But if a yellow sapphire is also tinged with red, it is known as kuraṇḍaka. And if a yellow sapphire is slightly tinged with blue, it is known as somanaka. A woman who does not have any son will give birth to one if she wears a yellow sapphire.

"Another type of jewel is named karketana (hessonite). It originated from Balāsura's nails. These nails fell into a bed of lotuses and there created this gem. Karketana can be of many colors, red, milky-white, yellow, copper-colored and blue. This jewel becomes brighter if it is wrapped in gold leaf and burnt in a fire. Karketana is a good jewel to wear if one wants to stay healthy or prolong one's life."

Appendix 3

Sanskrit Names of Various Gems

Sanskrit	Translit	English	Sanskrit	Translit	English
वज्र	vajra	Diamond	शशिकान्ता	śaśikāntā	Moonstone
इन्द्रनील	indranīla	Sky sapphire	सौगन्धिक	saugandhika	Lotus-Ruby
मरकत	marakata	Emerald	गोमेदक	gomedaka	Hessonite
कर्केतर	karketana	Chrysoberyl	शङ्ख	śaṅkha	Nacre
पद्मराग	padmarāga	Ruby	महानील	mahānīla	Blue sapphire
रुधिर	rudhira	Carnelian	पुष्पराग	puṣparāga	Yellow sapphire
वैदूर्य	vaidūrya	Cat's eye	ब्रह्ममणि	brahmamaṇi	Topaz
पुलक	pulaka	Garnet	ज्योतीरस	jyotīrasa	Agate
विमलक	vimalaka	Pyrite	सस्यक	sasyaka	Azurite
राजमणि	rājamaṇi	Red diamond	मुक्ता	muktā	Pearl
स्फटिक	sphaṭika	Rock Crystal	प्रवाल	pravāla	Red Coral

Alphabetic Index

17th century 5
21st century 1
Accident 52
Acid-cleaned 30
Acknowledgment vii
Affordable 23
Africa 26, 27
Agate 64
Airplanes 23
Alternative magazine 7
Aluminum 25, 29
Amalgamate 30
America 6, 12, 44, 49
Amplitude 41
Amulet 33
Ancient 1, 4, 6, 20, 34
Angle 11, 12, 14, 36, 39, 48, 53
Armed conflict 26
Arms 15, 27
Arrest 53
Aspirations 55
Asteroid 20, 21, 22
Astro 1, iii, 55
Astro Gem iii
Astrologer 5, 7, 8, 9, 12, 14, 19, 23, 32, 35, 36, 37, 38, 39, 40, 41, 42, 47, 51
Astrological 6, 16, 23, 24, 29, 31, 33, 50
Astrological "power" 23
Astrology 1, 4, 5, 6, 7, 9, 16, 28, 36
Astronomy 1, 5
Atom 22, 29, 57
Atomic 22
Atomic lattice 22
Attitude 8, 16
Aura 14, 15, 16, 18, 30, 45, 47
Auspicious 36, 50
Author 5, vii, 15, 40, 44, 59
Autobiography of a Yogi 16
Azurite 64
Babylonia 6
Bad luck 41, 52, 53, 54
Bad quality 62
Balancing 14
Balāsura 20, 61, 62, 63
Bamboos 62
Banker 9
Beautiful 9, 18, 40

Beauty 49
Belief 6, 16
Beryllium 25
Beryllium aluminum silicate 25
Best vii
Better destiny 16
Billionaire 9
Billions 8
Bird 56
Birefringence 25
Birth chart 8, 18, 19, 37
Birth data 10
Birth date 5, 8
Birth month 8, 18
Birth place 5, 8, 38
Birth stone 8, 18
Birth time 5, 8, 11, 51
Birthplace 11, 13
Black 29, 62
Black spots 29
Bliss 56, 57
Blood Diamond 24
Blue 1, 7, 17, 19, 21, 30, 61, 62, 63, 64
Blue sapphire 7, 17, 19, 21, 30, 61, 64
Bluish 25
Boars 62
Bodies 14, 62
Body 14, 15, 35, 36, 44, 45, 55, 56, 61, 62
Book 12, 15, 32, 59
Born 8, 11, 33, 63
Brahmamaṇi 64
Breath 8, 55
Breathing exercise 55
Brightness 34, 49
Brihat Pārāshara Horā Shāstra 36
Broach 53
Brother 3
Business 31, 42, 43
Byzantine 6
Calculate 1, 5, 8, 10, 39
Calculation 36
Calendar 8
Carat 3, 7, 9, 15, 18, 23, 31, 32, 33, 41, 42, 43, 44, 45, 46, 47, 51, 53, 60
Carats 47
Carats. 23

Career 8, 11, 33, 40
Carnelian 19, 61, 64
Cars 23
Cat's eye 17, 19, 21, 42, 51, 61, 63, 64
Cell 2, 15
Centuries 6
Ceramics 30
Chaotic 16
Character 5, 25
Charging 14
Cheaper 28, 31
Chemical 23, 25
Chemical Composition 23, 25
Children 11, 24, 33, 34, 39, 40, 56
Chrysoberyl 19, 61, 64
Civilization 1
Clarity 33
Cleanse 50
Cleavage 25
Client 15, 31, 37, 39, 41, 43, 45, 47, 48, 52
Clouds 57, 62
Coherence 55
Coherent 23
Coherent quantum field 23
Coldness 15
Color 1, 14, 22, 23, 26, 29, 30, 34, 47, 51, 53, 57, 61, 62, 63
Color Filter 26
Color Filter Reaction 26
Color variation 29
Color zone change 23
Combinations of gems 39
Comparison chart 24
Compatible 4
Conch-shells 62
Consciousness 55, 56, 57, 58
Constellation 6, 8, 11
Contentment 54
Contract 42, 53
Copper-colored 63
Coppery 61
Coral 17, 19, 30, 61, 64
Correct birth time 51
Correct gem 12, 36
Corundum 29, 30
Cosmic 1, 14, 47, 57

65

Cosmos 16
Couple 11, 51
Creation 20, 21, 27
Creativity 18
Crown 23, 33, 54
Crown jewels 23, 33
Crystal 19, 20, 21, 22, 23, 25, 29, 30, 31, 40, 59, 61, 64
Crystal lattice 23, 29, 31
Crystal structure 21, 29, 30, 31
Crystallization 20
Crystallized 20
Crystallographic Character 25
Culture 1
Dark space 57
Darkness 35
Dasha 50
Demon 20, 61
Deposits 20, 21
Destinies 8, 11
Destiny 1, 8, 11, 15, 16, 18, 23, 30, 32, 34, 36, 39, 41, 44, 45, 46, 47, 50, 52, 53, 55
Diamond 17, 19, 24, 26, 27, 44, 54, 61, 62, 64
Discoveries 3
Disorderly 30
Dispersion 25
Dog 56
Donkey 23, 47
Dreams 57
Dyes 30
Dynamics 4, 17
Early retirement 33
Earth 8, 11, 20, 21, 22, 46, 57, 58, 61
East 11
Ebay 32, 33
EBook 59
Ecliptic 17
Editor 7
Effect 1, 4, 8, 9, 12, 14, 15, 18, 26, 27, 29, 30, 31, 32, 33, 36, 38, 40, 41, 43, 45, 47, 49, 50, 51, 55
Effect of Acid 26
Effect of Heat 26
Electromagnetic 22
Electromagnetic field 22
Electron 27, 57

Elephants 62
Emerald 17, 18, 19, 24, 25, 27, 30, 31, 43, 45, 46, 61, 63, 64
Emitted 2
Energy 12, 14, 34
Energy field 12, 14
English 18, 31, 33, 43, 44, 51, 64
Enlightened 1, 55, 56, 57
Enlightenment 55, 56
Enrich 14, 46
Entrepreneur 43
Environment 1, 8, 23, 55, 56
Europe 6
Evaporating 21
Evolution of rock 27
Ewel 19, 31
Exact 1, 6, 8, 22, 23
Expensive 22, 33, 44
Experience 3, 5, 11, 15, 18, 19, 23, 32, 41, 43, 47, 52, 56
Expert 14
Factors 6, 8, 11
Fame 3
Famous 9, 40
Faults 31
Fear 51
Feet 15
Field 1, 4, 12, 14, 15, 16, 17, 18, 22, 23, 29, 35, 36, 39, 40, 41, 47
Filtered sunlight 49
Financial situation 43
Finger 48
Fire 31, 33, 63
First breath 8
First priority 32
Fishes 62
Flaw 23, 29, 30, 36
Forehead 15
Formula 1, 36
Fortunate 5, 6, 12, 38, 52
Fracture 23, 30
Fragments 21
Free will 32
Freedom 5, 55
Frequencies 16, 48
Frequency 1
Friday 17
Frien 39
Friend 39, 40, 51, 56, 57

Friendship 39
Friendship matrix 39
Fulfill your desires 32, 55
Fundamental 5, 38
Galaxy 57
Galilei 5
Garnet 19, 61, 64
Garuḍa 19, 31, 61, 62
Garuḍa Purāṇa 19, 31, 61
Gem 3, 9, 12, 13, 14, 15, 18, 22, 23, 24, 28, 29, 30, 31, 32, 35, 36, 38, 39, 40, 41, 42, 43, 45, 46, 47, 48, 49, 50, 51, 55, 63
Gem combination 38, 40
Gem consultation 18
Gem industry 24, 29
Gem size 15, 41, 45
Gem wholesaler 30
Gems 1, iii, 7, 8, 9, 11, 14, 15, 16, 17, 18, 19, 20, 22, 23, 24, 27, 28, 29, 30, 31, 32, 33, 34, 36, 37, 38, 39, 40, 41, 42, 43, 44, 45, 46, 47, 48, 50, 51, 52, 53, 54, 55, 64
Gems immediately. 9
Gemstone 1, 22, 48
General Assembly 26, 27
Geologist 20
Geometric 22
Geometric structure 22
Glass 21, 26, 29, 30
Globe 11, 12, 39
God consciousness 58
Gold 33, 34, 46, 47, 52, 53, 63
Golden 32, 53, 61
Gomedaka 17, 64
Good luck 41, 46, 53
Good partner 51
Good planet 36
Govern 1, 14, 40
Governing 1
Graha 36, 37, 39, 50, 52
Graha friendship 39
Gram 60
Gravitation 16
Greece 6
Green 1, 17, 25, 30, 63
Hand 15, 23, 30, 41, 50, 53
Happiness 8, 11, 32, 38, 56
Happy 18, 43, 46, 47

Hardness 25
Harm 4, 36, 37
Harmony 23, 55, 56
Headache 39
Health 9, 11, 32, 38, 43, 63
Heart 15, 54
Heat-treated 29, 30, 31
Heat-treating 30
Heat-treatment 30
Heaven 58
Heaven on Earth 58
Heavenly body 35, 36
Heavens 17
Herbs 63
Hessonite 17, 63, 64
Hexagonal 25, 62
High pressure 20
Highest quality gems 33
Highly orderly 23
Himalaya 63
History 55
Holiday 39
Holiness 49
Horoscope 5, 8, 10, 11, 12, 14, 32, 33, 35, 36, 38, 39, 40, 51, 52, 53, 55
Houses 33, 52
Human 4, 16, 37
Humanity 4
Hundreds of thousands 24
Hundreds of years 22
Ice cream 3
Immediate 15, 32, 33, 40, 42, 47, 53, 56, 57
Immortal 33
Impact 20, 21, 22
Inauspicious 36, 50
Inclusion 23, 30, 32, 33
Inclusions 33
Income 11, 18, 42
India 6, 27, 41, 43, 54
Indigo 1, 17
Individual 5, 6, 8, 10, 14, 15, 16, 18, 19, 23, 35, 36, 38, 39, 45, 47, 57
Individual birth chart 8, 18, 19
Indra 61, 62
Indranīla 19, 61, 63, 64
Industrialist 9
Infra-red 1, 17
Intelligent 9, 32
Intense pressure 21
Intensity 15

Internet 43
Intrinsic 22
IR 1
Jewel 17, 18, 19, 22, 23, 29, 31, 33, 42, 49, 52, 53, 61, 63
Jewelery industry 22
Jupiter 17, 50
Jyotīrasa 64
Jyotish 1, 4, 5, 6, 7, 18, 35, 37
Jyotishi 35
Karketana 19, 61, 63, 64
Karma 24, 42
Kepler 5
Ketu 17
King Henry the Sixth 54
Knowledge 5, 6, 8, 14, 28, 56, 57
Krug iii, iv, 59
Kuraṇḍaka 63
Lab-created 3, 9, 22, 23, 24, 25, 27, 31, 33, 42, 43, 44, 46, 51
Lab-grown 23
Laboratory-Grown 24, 25
Landlord 53
Laser 23, 31
Laser light 23, 31
Lattice 22, 23, 29, 31
Law of gravitation 16
Laws 1, 16, 21, 22, 23, 29, 41
Laws of nature 22
Lawyer 53
Life 1, 3, 5, 6, 7, 18, 20, 24, 27, 32, 34, 38, 40, 42, 43, 44, 45, 47, 50, 51, 52, 56, 57, 58, 63
Life period 50
Life style 42
Life threatening 24
Light 1, 2, 3, 14, 16, 22, 23, 31, 35, 41, 46, 47, 49, 50, 51, 55, 56, 57, 63
Light. 5
Literature 38
Lives 1, 8, 14, 47
Living 2, 5, 45, 55, 56, 57
Location 1, 11, 12, 38, 40
Location, 14
Lotus-Ruby 64
Lotuses 63
Loud speaker 41

Love 8, 43, 46, 57
Lucky stars 36
Lunar node 17, 36, 39, 50, 52
Magic 14, 46, 56
Magma 20, 21, 22
Mahānīla 17, 63, 64
Maharishi 7, 27, 28, 58
Maharishi Mahesh Yogi 7, 27, 58
Man-made gem 23
Mani 19, 61
Manipulation 30, 31
Manufactured 23
Marakata 17, 19, 61, 63, 64
Married 51
Mars 17
Masha 60
Master 1, 8, 16, 34
Materials 23
Mayor 40
Measuring 14
Medical doctor 39
Medicine 40
Medieval 6
Meditate 43, 55
Meditation 27, 55, 58
Mercury 17
Mesopotamia 6
Metal 47, 52, 53, 54
Milk 50, 62, 63
Milky-white 61, 63
Millionaire 9, 51
Millions of years 20, 22
Mind 3, 14, 51, 55, 57
Mines 24, 28, 63
Minimum gem size 15
Mining 24
Minutes 8, 15, 46
Misfortune 31, 62, 63
Misguided client 37
Modern 1, 4, 5
Mohs Scale 25
Molecular 29
Molecule 27, 28
Molten glass 21
Molten magma 20
Monday 17
Money 8, 23, 30, 43, 44
Months 3, 8, 14, 20, 22, 43, 51
Moon 11, 14, 17, 36, 39, 50, 52, 55

67

Moonstone 64
Morgan 9
Mountain 21, 61, 63
Muktā 17, 19, 61, 64
Multicolored 61
Myth 22
Nacre 64
Natural 20, 21, 22, 23, 24, 25, 28, 29, 30, 31, 32, 33, 36, 56
Natural gem 20, 22, 23, 24, 28, 29, 30, 31, 32, 33
Natural gem industry 24, 29
Natural gem mines 28
Natural laws 21
Necklace 53
Negative 4, 14, 24, 35, 38, 48, 52, 53
New millennium 29
Night 6, 11, 50, 62
Non-disturbed 23
North 12, 17
North America 12
Observation 57
Ocean 21, 62, 63
Oiled 30, 31
Old age 33
Opaque 26
Opportunities 8
Optical Character 25
Orange 1, 17
Orbit 17, 21
Original 1, 5, 7, 11, 27, 28, 38
Outwitting 16
Oyster 21, 62
Padmarāga 17, 19, 61, 62, 64
Paperback 59
Pārāshara 36, 38
Passion 8
Passport 45, 46
Past and future 56
Patañjali 57
Peace 27
Pearl 17, 19, 21, 61, 62, 64
Pendant 48
Period 14, 50, 52
Philosopher 49
Photograph 14
Photon 2
Physical being 1
Physicist 41, 57

Physiology 45
Place of birth 11
Place of residence 8, 9, 10, 12, 13, 19, 37
Planet 1, 4, 11, 14, 17, 20, 21, 35, 36, 37, 39, 40, 45, 50, 52, 55, 56, 57
Planet, s 8
Planetary 1, 4, 11, 14, 17, 36, 37, 40
Planetary friendship 40
Planetary strength 36
Pleochroism 25
Police 46, 52, 53
Police station 46, 52
Polished 27
Popp 2, 40
Position 23, 25, 32, 36
Positive 4, 11, 14, 27, 32, 35, 36, 37, 38, 41, 53, 55
Power 23, 24, 33, 35, 36, 41, 50, 51
Practic 41
Practical 27, 32, 41, 43, 45, 48
Pratikul 37
Pravāla 17, 19, 61, 64
Precaution 62
Precious gem 20
Precious metal 47
Precious stone 21, 61
Predicting 7
Prediction 5
Pressure 20, 21, 23
Price 23, 30
Prismatic 25
Processing 31
Property speculator 33
Pulaka 19, 61, 64
Purāṇa 19, 20, 21, 31, 61
Purity 22
Purple 29
Puṣparāga 17, 19, 61, 63, 64
Pyrite 64
Quality 23, 25, 31, 33, 37, 62
Quantum 1, 4, 14, 15, 16, 17, 18, 23, 29, 35, 36, 39, 41, 47
Quantum field 1, 4, 14, 15, 16, 17, 18, 23, 29, 35, 36, 39, 41, 47
Quartz 19, 61

Radiation 4
Rahu 17
Rainbow 1, 17
Rājamaṇi 64
Ranslation 34, 42
Ratti 41, 60
Rāvaṇa 62
Rebel groups 26
Recommendation 12, 18, 19, 38, 39
Recommended 9, 33, 55
Red 1, 17, 21, 26, 29, 30, 61, 62, 63, 64
Refractive 25, 30
Refractive index 25, 30
Religious 5, 49
Relocated 11, 18, 19, 37, 38
Relocated birth chart 18
Relocated chart 38
Relocation 1, 11, 38, 40
Relocation, 14
Rental agreement 53
Rental contract 53
Research 1, 6, 7, 31, 35, 40, 57
Residence 8, 9, 10, 12, 13, 19, 37
Resonate 22
Responsibility 58
Restoring peace 27
Richest 31
Rights iv
Ring 48
Rings 53
Rishikesh 27
River 21, 62
Romaharshaṇa 19, 31, 61
Rubies 21, 29, 30, 31, 62
Ruby 3, 9, 17, 19, 23, 29, 41, 61, 62, 64
Rudhira 19, 61, 64
Sage 38, 53, 55
Saline water 62
Sanskrit 1, 5, 17, 36, 38, 50, 56, 64
Sanskrit Name 17, 64
Sapphire 7, 17, 19, 21, 27, 29, 30, 31, 32, 33, 44, 50, 53, 61, 63, 64
Sasyaka 64
Saturday 17
Saturn 17
Saugandhika 64

School 40
Science 1, 4, 5, 6, 7, 14, 37
Scientific 6, 16, 20, 24, 27, 40
Scientific insight 40
Scientist 1, 3, 5, 7, 27
Scratch marks 48
Seconds 8
Secret 1, iii, 4, 5, 7, 8, 10, 11, 12, 14, 16, 17, 18, 19, 20, 21, 22, 28, 29, 31, 32, 34, 35, 36, 37, 38, 40, 41, 42, 43, 44, 45, 46, 47, 49, 50, 51, 52, 54, 55, 58
Selection of gems 18
Self esteem 40
Sensitive 14
Set of gems 19
Setting 47, 48
Shakespeare 54
Shastra 36
Shāstra 36
Side effect 38, 40
Sidereal 6
Sidhi 56, 57
Silicate 25
Silver 47
Sister 3
Size of the gem 15
Skin 30, 40, 47, 49, 63
Sky 6, 11, 61, 62, 64
Snake 62
Snakes 62
Solar system 1, 4, 17
Somanaka 63
Soul 14
Sound 1, 21, 41
South 17, 39
South Asian 39
Space ship 20
Space traveler 20
Space vehicle 61
Specific Gravity 25
Spectrum 1
Sphaṭika 19, 61, 64
Spiritual 32, 42, 43, 55
Splendor 34
Spots 29
Square law 41, 43
Sri Yukteswar 16
Star 6, 11
Stars 4, 16, 36, 56
Starter gem 43
Statistical 6
Stomach 15, 62
Stone 1, 8, 15, 18, 21, 22, 23, 27, 37, 45, 48, 54, 61, 64
Strength 5, 11, 14, 34, 35, 36, 37, 38
Strengthen 11, 14, 35, 36, 37, 38
Structure 21, 22, 29, 30, 31
Student 19, 31, 61
Study 4, 36
Success 8
Suffering 24, 28, 62
Sun 11, 14, 17, 18, 20, 21, 34, 36, 39, 47, 49, 50, 52, 55, 62
Sunday 17
Sunlight 14, 16, 47, 49, 51
Sunrise 11
Superficial 38
Supermarket 57
Supernatural 56
Superstition 41
Superstitious 24
Symmetrical 23
Systematic 1
Taylor 44
Teaching 12
Technological 23
Temperature 20, 22, 29, 30
Tensions 39
Testimonial 23
Thailand 32
Thousands of years 1, 6
Thursday 17
Thurston iii, iv, 59
Time 1, 3, 5, 6, 8, 11, 13, 14, 18, 22, 24, 41, 42, 43, 47, 50, 51, 52, 53, 56, 57, 59, 61
Times 34
Timing 8
Tola 60, 62
Topaz 19, 61, 64
Totality 12, 47
Toughness 25
Traditional 14, 24
Training 14
Translation 38, 46
Transparency 26
Transparency to X-Rays
Treasure 9, 46
Tropical 6
True 6, 16, 23, 35, 36, 63
Tuesday 17
TV 3
Twelve houses 52
Twins 8
Types of jewels 19, 61
Ultraviolet 1, 26
Understanding 1
Uni-axial 25
United Nations 26, 27
Unity consciousness 56
Universe 1, 57
Unlucky 39
Untrue 6
Upper limit 45, 46
UV 1
Vaidūrya 17, 19, 61, 63, 64
Vajra 17, 19, 61, 64
Valuable 23, 29, 62
Veda 5, 19, 31, 34, 42, 46, 61
Veda Vyāsa 19, 31, 61
Vedic 1, 4, 5, 6, 7, 8, 9, 14, 19, 20, 32, 35, 36, 37, 38, 51
Vedic astrologer 7, 8, 9, 14, 19, 32, 35, 38, 51
Vedic astrology 4, 5, 6, 7
Vedic civilization 1
Vedic Mathematics 7
Vedic Science 37
Vedic scripture 36
Vedic tradition 20
Venus 17
Very expensive 22, 44
Vibration 1, 14, 15, 22, 41
Vidura 63
Vimalaka 64
Vimāna 61
Violet 1, 17, 26
Visible 11, 22, 47, 56
Volume 41
Vyāsa 19, 31, 61
Warmth 15
Water 21, 50, 62
Wave function 23
Weak planet 36
Wealth 5, 11, 24, 32, 38, 43
Wearer 62
Wearing 1, 3, 9, 36, 37, 39, 2640, 47, 52, 53, 55, 62
Wednesday 17
Weekday 17
Weeks 18, 20, 22, 44

69

Weight 41, 42, 60, 62
Weight Measures 60
Well-being 32
West 5, vii, 11
West coast 12
Westbrook vii
Western 5, 6, 7
Wine 62
World peace 27
Wrong gem 52

X-Ray Fluorescence 26
Yajna 61
Year-old 3, 9, 18, 31, 33, 40, 42, 51, 52
Yellow 1, 17, 19, 30, 32, 33, 50, 53, 61, 63, 64
Yellow sapphire 17, 19, 30, 32, 33, 50, 53, 61, 63, 64
Yoga 4, 16, 55
Yogananda 4, 16

Zenith 11
Zodiac 6, 8, 18
  1, 3, 7, 9, 12, 15, 18, 24, 26, 31, 33, 36, 39, 42, 43, 45, 48, 51, 52, 56
"imitation" stones 23
Śaṅkha 64
Śaśikāntā 64

www.ingramcontent.com/pod-product-compliance
Lightning Source LLC
Chambersburg PA
CBHW042057290426
44112CB00001B/8